CW00728700

Max.

TAKING LIFE
AS IT COMES

With Best Wishes
from
Ben Bibby

Ben Bibby

with illustrations by
Lucy Reynolds

© **2011 Ben Bibby**
Taking Life as it Comes

ISBN 978-0-9569778-0-9

Published by Ben Bibby
Tŷ'n Cae
Brynsiencyn
Llanfairpwllgwyngyll
Anglesey LL61 6HJ

The right of Ben Bibby to be identified as the author of this work and Lucy Reynolds as the illustrator have been asserted by them in accordance with the Copyright, Designs and Patents Act 1988.

All rights reserved. No part of this publication may be produced in any form or by any means – graphic, electronic or mechanical including photocopying, recording, taping or information storage and retrieval systems – without the prior permission, in writing, of the publisher.

A CIP catalogue record of this book
can be obtained from the British Library.

Book designed by Michael Walsh at
THE BETTER BOOK COMPANY
5 Lime Close • Chichester PO19 6SW

and printed by
IMPRINTDIGITAL.NET
Seychelles Farm • Upton Pyne • Exeter EX5 5HY

AUTHOR'S FOREWORD
and
ACKNOWLEDGEMENTS

90% of the content of this book is derived from two collections of verse, *A Birthday Ode and Other Verse* and *A Letter to a Grandson and Other Verse*, which were printed for private circulation in 1994. The remaining 10% consists of poems written since 1994. For various reasons some of the poems from the original collections have been omitted and those included have been slightly altered in many cases.

I would like to acknowledge the help I have received from:

My daughter, Lindsay, who was the first to suggest that poems originally written for the amusement of my family were worthy of a wider audience.

My friend Michael Harrison who encouraged me in the belief that at least some of my work was worthy of publication and helped me in many ways, including occasional censorship, when I was writing *A Birthday Ode* and *A Letter to a Grandson*, but, sadly, did not live to make what I am sure would have been a similar contribution to the present book.

My great-niece, Lucy Reynolds, who supplied the illustrations.

My younger son, William, whose expertise in computer software has helped me to solve innumerable problems.

Michael Walsh, who since I first approached *The Better Book Company* in August 2008, has guided me painstakingly through the intricacies of publication and has born with patience the interruption caused by my move from West Kirby to Anglesey.

Ben Bibby
September 2011
Tŷ'n Cae

CONTENTS

THE POET AT HOME

The poems in this section were written between 1989 and 1994 and with the exception of 'Ode to Susan on her Fifty-Sixth Birthday' and 'An Old Photograph', which is a flashback to the poet's national service in the army, they describe the ageing process as it affects the poet, his wife and their cat, Pharaoh. This culminates in a contemplation of the implications of grand-father-hood followed by a letter to the grandson, James, who was born in Auckland, New Zealand, in May 1994.

ODE TO SUSAN ON HER FIFTY-SIXTH BIRTHDAY

Darling, you aren't growing old,
No silver threads among your gold.
'Twould be enough if you just stayed that way,
But you keep looking younger every day.

Your silk-smooth skin's the envy of your peers.
Your hair's cut short to show your shell-like ears.
My presbyopic eyes no wrinkles see,
When through bifocal lens I gaze on thee.

Your figure trim, with neither busk nor stay,
Defies the calories of Sharrow Bay,
And when from thence you climb the fells remote,
You are more nimble than a mountain goat.

When Neptune calls you to the Menai Strait,
Tide, wind and waves upon you wait.
Whether on runs, on reaches or on beats,
You are the undisputed mistress of the sheets.

In culinary circles you're the cream,
Your beef most rare, your chicken more supreme.
For just one taste a bishop would give his crozier.
Gods who have supped with you disdain ambrosia.

Fair roses bloom at your behest.
Your raspberries always fruit the best,
And brassicas more gladly grow,
When you have set them in their row.

There's scarce a skill and scarce an art,
At which you cannot play your part.
Your only weakness is your spelling,
And even that I find compelling.

But beauty, strength and skill are but the start,
What matters most is in your heart.
There is no essence for creating you.
You are one-off, unique, my only Sue.

AN OLD PHOTOGRAPH

Sue has just found this old photograph
In the bottom of a drawer,
So I don't think I can have shown it to you before,
But do tell me if I'm being a bore.
It was the first time a member of the Royal Family
Had visited Northern Ireland since before the war,
So it's really quite a historic photograph,
And appeared in the *Belfast Telegraph*.

That's me in the rear rank, nineteenth from the right.
It took me some time to find myself,
Even with the help of a magnifying glass and a good light.
I was only eighteen and a half,
But I thought I would have looked a little bit older.
Do you see where there are two military policemen
Keeping the crowds back? That's me,
With one of them standing just behind my right shoulder.

Our Platoon Commander is the one standing out in front;
He's wearing battle-dress and a beret like the rest of us
And you can't make out his badges of rank,
But you can tell he's an officer because he's got a revolver
In a webbing holster on his left hip.
In front of him, off the photo, were the bows of the ship.

Our Sergeant is the little man acting as rear right marker.
We thought he was a real bastard,
But really his bark was worse than his bite, and he probably
Only behaved so aggressively
To compensate for his lack of height.
He was called Sergeant Miles
And he was the best sergeant in the Company
And could reduce any man to tears.
Isn't it amazing that I can remember his name
After nearly fifty years?

He had been rehearsing us for the Guard-of-Honour
Every day for a week.

His voice was piercing and shrill rather than deep,
And with him giving the commands
We could have presented arms in our sleep.

Unfortunately, on the day,
The commands were the Platoon Commander's responsibility,
And although he had some military capability.
He didn't have Sergeant Miles' audibility.

So a movement we would have executed with precision
If we could have heard the command,
Was carried out with hesitation and indecision,
And we all thought it was a shambles, and pretty absurd
That a whole week's practice had been wasted
Because an officer hadn't practised making himself heard.

Probably nobody else except us noticed,
And if they had noticed they couldn't have cared less,
Because, as you can see, they were all too busy
Climbing onto roofs and scaffolding
To get a better view of the Princess.

That's her, walking along the front rank
With the Company Commander, followed by the top brass.
She obviously isn't looking at us,
Which makes calling it an inspection a bit of a farce.

When she walked along the rear rank,
She could have spoken to me
If she had wanted to. But she didn't.
And it was probably just as well,
Because I hadn't polished up my repartee.
I had never spoken to a Princess,
Even one quite a bit younger than me.

But I noticed that even in her high heels
She was rather small,
And she wore so much make-up
You couldn't tell what her face was really like at all.

Then she climbed onto a platform
And said something which we couldn't hear,
Because the crowd had all started to cheer,
And pulled a lever to release a bottle of champagne.

As the ship started to move down the ways,
The crowd shouted more hoorays,
And we presented arms again.

So that's the story, more or less,
Of how I got my picture in the *Belfast Telegraph*
And nearly spoke to a Princess.

And it's nice to have this old photograph as a reminder
That at Harland & Wolff's yard on 16th October 1947,
When *Edinburgh Castle* began her journey to the sea,
One of the soldiers presenting arms was me.

BIRTH OF A RECIPE

On the still summer eve,
Which did inspire this ballad,
Sue barbecued some lamb to serve
With baked potatoes and a salad.

There is some mayonnaise,
So, in my spoon I dig.
At least I thought 'twas mayonnaise,
Though the bowl seemed rather big.

The texture was, I saw,
A little grainy.
'The stupid woman's curdled it.' I thought,
'Why can't she be more brainy?'

The taste was tart,
And had a pleasing zip.
'Not mayonnaise!' I realized,
'Perhaps her latest dip!'

She saw it on my plate
And out did blurt,
'That isn't mayonnaise, nor yet a dip,
But our dessert.'

'Whate'er it be,'
I passed a dripping tasting-spoon in her direction,
'It complements burnt lamb
To rare perfection.'

We tasted late into the night,
And she at last agreed that I was right.
A recipe had been quite accidentally born,
Which left redcurrants and mint sauce a bit forlorn.

'I would be on the road' she said,
'To gastronomic fame,
If, "Sue's burnt lamb and gooseberry fool"
Was a more euphonious name.'

A LITTLE HARD OF HEARING

I have become a little deaf,
Though mainly in the treble clef.
I do not grieve. Nay! I rejoice,
I cannot hear the female voice
And have a ready-made excuse
For ignoring instructions and abuse.

There's not much problem with the bass,
So with men it is a different case.
Their words are usually quite clear
And I hear just what I want to hear,
Provided that they speak up loud
And are not in a noisy crowd.

But when I listen to CDs,
Enjoying music at my ease,
I turn the volume up quite high
And stand the speakers quite close by,
Then, with a touch of treble gain,
My hearing's perfect once again.

ALCOHOLICS ANOMALOUS

Sue complains that I'm a teeny
Bit too fond of dry Martini
And, when we both sit down to dine,
Drink more than my fair share of wine.

These accusations I've denied,
But I shall swallow up my pride
And try a bit of compromise
To raise my standing in her eyes.

My plan is this. I will forsake
The next Martini I might take,
My drinking habits rearrange,
Try a dry sherry for a change,
And, when we next sit down to dine,
Give her her own carafe of wine.

ON TRYING TO OPEN A PACKET OF BISCUITS

Is it one which you open
By pulling a microscopic piece of red plastic?
Or one where you have to do something more drastic?
Or one where the instructions for opening
Are in very small print underneath,
And you only see them
After you've opened it with your teeth?
Or one where the instructions begin,
'Take the packet out of the deep freeze'
And from there on are incomprehensible
Because they've been so badly translated
From the Japanese?

And why is it that if it's one
Where you have to prise up one of the corners
With your finger-nail.
It's always the last corner you try
And also your last finger-nail?

Compared with this plastic bubble,
Getting into one of the old-fashioned sardine cans
Was no trouble,
Unless you'd lost the key.
In which case you either used the key off another can
Or did without sardines for tea.

I realize that there may be good reasons
For making some packaging child-proof,
But the reason for making it adult-proof
I've not yet been told.
But I do know
That if you want a packet of biscuits opened quickly,
The best way is to give it to a five-year-old.

I think I've cracked it.
This is one where you have to stick
A sharp-pointed knife
In there and then lever that bit up to extract it.
Blast!
Now I'm going to have to ask Sue to try to open
A packet of Elastoplast.

PHARAOH

We have a cat called Pharaoh,
Of whom Sue makes a fuss.
We like to think we own him,
But he knows he owns us.

He is an Abyssinian,
And has a pedigree.
There are no low-born moggies
In Pharaoh's family tree.

He comes when Susan calls him,
But comes at his own pace,
To show that he's superior,
And keep her in her place.

If meals are late at Kirby Mount,
He goes next door to Ann,
Who is always more than willing
To open him a can.

I always give him breakfast,
But he never talks to me,
Unless I need reminding
That it is time for tea.

Though sometimes, to show gratitude,
He brings us in a mouse
And lays it out to please us
In some corner of the house.

When he was young and agile,
He kept the garden clear
And fought with any other cat,
Who came a bit too near.

Now he is old and rather stiff
And emphysemic too,
He can't see off the neighbours'cats,
The way he used to do.

He lies there in his basket,
Sleeping the time away,
And sometimes won't go out at all,
If it's a rainy day.

We hope he'll still be with us,
For several years to come,
And come and lie beside us
And let us stroke his tum.

We're very fond of Pharaoh,
He's nice to have around,
And Kirby Mount won't be the same,
When Pharaoh's underground.

LA DIFFÉRENCE

A poet
Is a genius and wants you to know it,
So he makes everything long-winded and obscure,
Even when he is writing about *la belle amour*.

Whereas a writer of verse
Thinks that obscurity is rather perverse,
So he makes everything brief and clear
And has *deux pieds sur la terre*.

So, in a piece describing a cat,
A poet would say, at great length, that
It embodied the spirit of the Sphinx
And had other Ancient Egyptian links.

Whereas a writer of verse
Would be more terse,
And would say that it had a loud purr,
Four legs, sharp claws, a face, a tail and fur.

THE POET LOOKS INTO HIS MIRROR
ON HIS SIXTY-FIFTH BIRTHDAY

Is this the face that I have seen before?
The self-same visage that I knew of yore!
I thought it would have changed a little more,
Now that I am no longer sixty-four.

I have survived to draw my modest pension,
And to continue to is my intention.
I see no signs of gout or hypertension,
Or other worse afflictions I could mention.

My spectacles, though frequently mislaid,
I need more often than my hearing aid.
My hair, though thin, is only slightly greyed.
The teeth still left are not too much decayed.

I can still walk without the aid of sticks,
Though slightly rusty at my party tricks.
In low society I do not mix.
I hope I can survive to sixty-six.

ON REALIZING THE IMPLICATIONS
OF BECOMING A GRANDFATHER

I'm going to be a grandpa,
Or so the stars foretell.
One never can be certain.
Let's hope that all goes well.

She could be a lovely little girl.
He could be quite a boy.
Whichever way God wills it,
I'll still be filled with joy.

Polish your brass ye trumpeters,
Practise your rolls ye drums,
Prepare to sound a fanfare,
The day my grandchild comes.

But wait, I've just remembered,
Each lining has its cloud,
So mute the trumpets slightly,
Don't let them play too loud.

Sound fanfares in a minor key,
Muffle your rolls ye drums,
For my wife becomes a granny,
The day my grandchild comes.

A LETTER TO A GRANDSON

'Aboard, aboard, for shame!
The wind sits in the shoulder of your sail,
And you are stayed for.'

Polonius' words are aptly set
To start this letter to you, grandson I've never met,
For soon you will be sailing 'cross the Indian Ocean
Drinking your mother's milk, stirred by its gentle motion.
You soon will have more sailing miles in your life's log,
Than has your grandpa, though an old sea-dog.

Polonius speaks again.

'There, my blessing with thee
And these few precepts in thy memory.'

For though you cannot read this letter, writ in my own hand,
I'll ask your mother please to keep it safe,
And read it to you when she thinks you'll understand.

Be slow to speak and choose your words with care,
And never with bad language foul the air.
Pick your friends carefully, keep your friendships bright,
But waste no time on ships that pass at night.
Don't go round picking fights, but, if you have to fight,
Fight hard and get your blows in where they hurt.
Then, when he's down, stand back, your self-control regain.
You'll find he won't pick fights with you again.
Play games to win, rejoice in ordered strife,
But don't forget that games are not the goal of life.
You will not always win the race, but never whine.
Congratulate the victor on the line.
Listen to what men say and well-meant criticism take
And ponder on its worth.
A friend prepared to say, 'Thou doest wrong.'
Is the best friend on earth.
Wear decent clothes, appropriate to the work in hand.
Respect the customs of each foreign land.
Wash daily, don't forget to comb or brush your hair,
For people can be judged by how they may appear.

Neither an idler nor a wastrel be,
For slacking dulls the edge of industry.
Work hard and pass on to another generation
All that is best in family and in nation.

Polonius speaks once more. I cannot put it better,
His words began and they will end this letter.

'This above all: to thine own self be true,
And it must follow, as the night the day,
Thou canst not then be false to any man.'

Farewell, dear grandson, till the day we meet,
Sleep soundly and may all your dreams be sweet,
And flights of angels sing thee to thy rest,
And don't forget your Dad and Mum know best.

PS. Remind your Dad and Mum to hold you tight,
And clip your harness on, on deck at night.

ROUND THE WORLD

The first three poems in this section were written during a voyage round the world on which the poet's elder son, John, and his wife, Lou, and his younger son, Will, and his partner, Nicky, embarked in their yacht, 'Conder', in November 1991. The poet and his wife, Sue, and their daughter, Lindsay, and son-in-law, Justin, and other relations and friends joined them for some legs of the voyage.

'Henry the Wahoo' was written after a leg from Grenada to Bonaire, an island in the Netherlands Antilles. 'His Majesty King Taufa'Ahau Tupoe 1V' was written after a cruise through the Tongan archipelago and 'South Island Blues' was written after a tour of New Zealand's South Island which was preceded and followed by cruising off the East Coast of North Island.

William and Nicky left 'Conder' shortly after arriving in New Zealand. They married and settled in Seattle where William was working when the poet and Sue visited them and 'Lines Inspired by a Notice on an American Golf Course' was written.

HENRY THE WAHOO

He came up from astern off Tortuga,
In response to Louise's (al)lures,
And, after a long-drawn resistance,
Came aboard to form part of our stores.

He was recognised soon as a wahoo,
A game-fish and gastronome's treat.
At thirty pounds weight he was fated
To provide us with plenty to eat.

We put in to a small sandy island,
Which took us a few hours to reach.
Will sharpened his knives up for filleting,
While John lit a fire on the beach.

Soon Henry was all neatly packaged,
And ready to lay on the ice.
His remains were discreetly disposed of,
And the sharks ate them up in a trice.

John selected some cuts for oak-smoking.
The results were a real *tour de force*.
They made a delicious lunch menu,
With salad and horseradish sauce.

Will took over the galley for dinner,
And with Delia Smith as his guide,
He cooked us 'Italian Baked Fish',
And served it with justified pride.

The result was pronounced quite delicious,
And was set off with nicely chilled wine,
Which Nicky with care had selected,
And poured out when we sat down to dine.

We sailed overnight to Los Roques,
And arrived with a ravenous crew.
So the Magimix swung into action,
And a pâté was knocked up by Lou.

We ate it for lunch with great gusto,
On toast, with a shandy or two.
It only needs cream cheese and lemon,
Provided you've caught your wahoo.

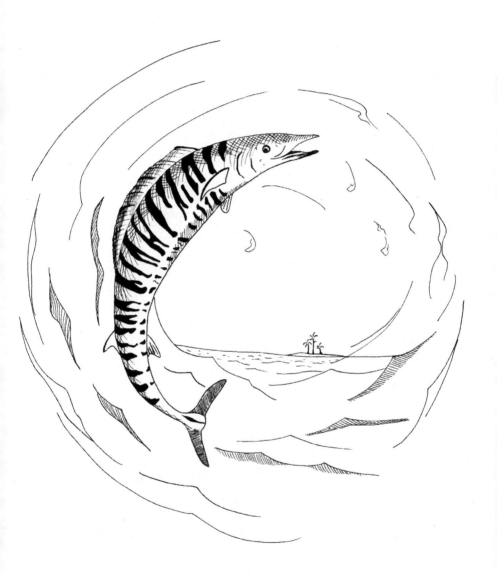

For dinner, Will barbecued chicken.
We felt Henry had earned one night's rest.
But next lunch time we couldn't resist him,
And we ate some more pâté with zest.

That night was the turn of the old hands,
So Sue made a fish pie, which then
Was topped with a light mashed potato,
A unique contribution from Ben.

We sailed for Los Aves next morning,
Sotovento (The Isle on the Lee).
And we tried to forget about Henry.
There are other fish in the sea.

We bade final farewell when we anchored,
And we did so with tears in each eye,
Consoled by the choice on the menu,
Of pâté or warmed-up fish pie.

But now we are parting from *Conder*,
For at last we've arrived in Bonaire.
We look back on two weeks of pure pleasure,
As we wash out the salt from our hair.

We remember the climb on Testigos,
To the light on its cactus-ringed peak,
And the magical world under water,
Where parrot-fish play hide-and-seek.

We remember the long-legged flamingos,
Taking off from the salt-pans last night,
Wheeling high overhead in formation,
Then abruptly aborting their flight.

We wish the crew well as we leave them,
To follow their west-going trail,
While we fly back home towards sunrise,
With instructions for posting Lou's mail.

Sue worries of course for their future,
As mothers invariably do.
But she knows they've no fear of starvation,
Provided they catch a wahoo.

HIS MAJESTY KING TAUFA'AHAU TUPOE IV

Tonga has a mighty king,
Good at almost everything.
He weighs in at thirty stone
And needs a specially strengthened throne.

Hidden from the common masses
Behind a pair of Ray-Ban glasses,
He presides at all the shows
And whatever he says goes.

Before him, when the speeches end,
The dancing girls in lines extend,
Displaying all their teenage charms
And miming with their well-oiled arms

They're followed by the dancing-boys,
Who stamp their feet and make a noise,
With paddle-spears pretend to kill,
Like orchestrated bayonet drill.

The king just sits and never moves.
You can't tell whether he approves.
He's seen it many times before.
I guess he finds it all a bore.

Envoi:

His kingdom's good he has at heart
And he plays a twentieth-century part.
His ancestors gained fame by fighting.
He'll be remembered for street-lighting.

This verse was inspired by visits to the Vava'i agricultural show in Neiafu, The Ha'apai agricultural show in Pangai and a tour of Tongatapu during which we saw three plaques commemorating the completion of street-lighting projects.

SOUTH ISLAND BLUES

We had studied basic Kiwi
And had mastered, 'There you go',
And, Thanks to Lou, already knew
What is meant by 'BYO'.
We had figured out, 'No Exit'
As we journeyed through the land,
But had bought no 'pre-loved' clothing.
(It just means, 'second-hand'.)
We had travelled to the Southern Lakes
And there we saw unfold
A vast adventure-playground
For the seriously old.

Its centre is at Queenstown,
A place on pleasure bent.
You needn't bring equipment,
For there's nothing you can't rent.
It catered in the gold-rush days
For miners at their play,
But the gold was soon exhausted
And they left it to decay,
Till the citizens discovered
A second seam of gold,
Selling instant second childhood
To the seriously old.

There's no discrimination
Of colour, race or creed;
By car and coach and aeroplane,
To Queenstown they all speed.
They come from far-off places,
To frolic at their ease,
Aussies and Brits and Germans,
But mostly Japanese,
And all of them are welcome,
Provided they bring gold,
Or a reputable credit card,
And are seriously old.

South Island Blues

You can fish for trout or salmon,
With a rod in either hand,
Or lie beside the pool
And get your wrinkled torso tanned.
You can take a sunset cruise
Aboard a steamer on the lake,
And buy Maori carvings
Which are probably all fake.
But the pleasure of these pastimes
Has been greatly oversold,
And you need much more excitement
When you're seriously old.

You can dress up in a track-suit
And jog for half a mile,
Then take a Finnish sauna
And a massage, Swedish style.
You can ride a mountain bicycle,
With multitudes of gears,
And use forgotten muscles,
Which you haven't used for years.
But after careful thinking,
We put both of these on hold,
For you have to work up slowly
When you're seriously old.

You can always try aerobics,
To pass the time of day,
But remember water-ski-ing
Is just a bit *passé*.
But of all these healthy pastimes,
The one we sampled first
Was a tour of local vineyards
To satisfy our thirst.
We thought this was essential,
As so often we've been told,
You should not get dehydrated
When you're seriously old.

South Island Blues

We thought about jet-boating,
But it seemed a noisy sport,
And we have never seen ourselves
As quite the jet-set sort.
We scorned white-water rafting.
It doesn't take much skill.
We watched the bungee-jumping,
But it made us both feel ill.
Throwing yourself off bridges,
Just to show that you are bold,
Is hardly the behaviour
Of the seriously old.

We'd already tried kayaking
With a sympathetic guide,
Who kept Sue from capsizing
By rafting at her side,
Until she'd gained her confidence
And paddled at her best,
Snug in her skin-tight wet-suit,
Over her thermal vest,
A sensible precaution
For warding off the cold,
For exposure can be dangerous
When you're seriously old.

We'd already looked at glaciers,
So we crossed them off our list.
There are no whales in Queenstown
To replace the whales we'd missed.
At soaring snow-capped mountains
We'd had a first-class look,
For we'd flown by helicopter
Past the summit of Mount Cook.
We sought some new adventure,
As time relentless rolled.
There's no time for repetition,
When you're seriously old.

South Island Blues

We decided upon climbing,
Which we'd trained for on the way,
So we clambered up Ben Lomond
On a hot and sunny day.
We admit we took the gondola
For fifteen hundred feet,
But even so we thought our climb
A memorable feat.
So proudly we decided
That our children must be told,
That we're capable of climbing
Though we're seriously old.

But, alas, too soon approached for us
The end of our short stay,
And we could not agree on
The adventure of the day,
So eventually decided
Each would take a separate course,
Ben on a paraglider
And Sue upon a horse.
And it wasn't that we'd quarrelled,
Nor had our love turned cold,
But one needs one's independence,
When one's seriously old.

The day dawned bright and sunny,
But Ben heard the pundits say,
'The wind's in the wrong direction
And rain is on the way.
It isn't fit for flying.
You're grounded I'm afraid
But of course we will refund you
The money you have paid.
This left Ben with a problem,
He was left out in the cold,
And a day cannot be wasted,
When you're seriously old.

South Island Blues

He ran to the nearest office,
Where adventures could be booked,
And through the piles of brochures,
He feverishly looked,
Till his eyes lit on a brochure,
At which his spirits soared,
A swim down the Kawarau
On a polystyrene board.
This may sound rather flimsy,
But at least it can't be holed,
And is buoyant body-armour
For the seriously old.

A van arrived in minutes
And Ben soon was on the shore,
In flippers and a wet-suit
With half a dozen more
Intrepid river-surfers,
All listening to their guide.
'Keep close to me.' He told them,
'There are rocks on either side.
Don't get into back-eddies
And do as you are told.
For we can't turn back to rescue
The seriously old.'

They launched into the river
And there displayed their skills,
Shooting a few small rapids
With only minor spills.
Ben ran into a cliff face
And came off second-best,
But this was only practice
For the object of their quest,
The infamous Chinese dog-leg,
Which, so they had been told,
Was a trap for the unwary
And the seriously old.

South Island Blues

Two minutes of confusion,
Of roaring, rushing foam,
Belatedly Ben realised
That he should have stayed at home.
He had to paddle frantically,
Exerting all his strength,
Missing a rocky promontory
By less than half a length.
He reached the shore eventually,
Exhausted, stiff and cold,
And they said, 'You should have told us
You were seriously old.'

Meanwhile Sue had been enjoying
Her *Moonlight Stables* ride,
Along a pleasant bridle-path
Close by the river's side.
They had put her on a race-horse,
(Though many years retired),
And her fearless headlong gallop
Was very much admired.
And when they had retrieved her,
She was very soon consoled,
When they said, 'We never guessed
That you were seriously old'

Later they met in Queenstown,
To relate how they had fared.
Ben's limbs still felt like jelly;
He admitted he'd been scared.
Sue was most relieved to see him
And was glad he wasn't dead,
And showed him all the places,
Where her legs had been rubbed red.
For she seemed to have forgotten,
Though she certainly was told,
That you ought to ride in Jodhpurs,
When you're seriously old.

South Island Blues

The moral of this story
Should really be quite plain,
But just in case you've missed it,
I'll repeat it once again.
If Ben wants to reach his century
He must lead a quiet life,
And heed the admonitions
Of his ever-loving wife.
His brain may be quite nimble
And his spirit may be bold,
But his body just can't take it
Now he's seriously old.

PACKING FOR A HOLIDAY
ON A TROPICAL ISLAND

(Lines Written After Three Rainy Days in the Seychelles)

Before you pack for a holiday
In a tropical paradise,
I hope you'll read this piece of verse.
It contains some good advice.

You'll spend your days on a sandy beach,
And there you'll only wear
A bathing suit. Pack two or three
And plenty of *Ambre Solaire*.

Sunglasses, T shirts, floppy hats,
Sandals and books to read
Complete the essential tropical kit,
Which you by day will need.

For evening, women need some skirts
Or sarongs, perhaps a dress.
Some take as many as three or four,
The wise get by on less.

Never, (as foolish women do,
Though staying for but a week),
Take as many changes of evening wear
As would stock a small boutique.

Men need some light-weight trousers
And shirts. (I suggest drip dry.)
They never need a jacket,
Nor yet an old school tie.

Informality is 'in' these days,
So do not overdress.
Strive for an air of *savoir faire*
And studied casualness.

For most hot destinations,
This should put you on the track,
But for any spells in the Seychelles,
There is one more thing to pack.

For in those isles it rains a lot,
So women as well as fellers,
Should be sure to place, in a handy case,
The largest of their umbrellas.

But even in those rainy isles,
The sun will shine at last.
The sky will become the brightest blue,
No longer overcast.

Once more you'll idle on the beach,
Prone on your lounger loll,
And a large umbrella, you will find,
Makes an ideal parasol.

FAISANT VOS BAGAGES POUR LES VACANCES
SUR UNE ÎLE TROPICALE

(Lignes Écrites Après Trois Jours Pluvieux aux Séchelles)

Avant de faire vos bagages,
Pour un paradis au soleil,
Lisez ce poème, je vous en prie.
Il contient des bons conseils.

Sur la plage vous passerez les jours,
(Pas autre chose à faire!)
Prenez des maillots, deux ou trois,
Et beaucoup d'*Ambre Solaire*.

Lunettes et chapeaux de soleil,
Sandales, T shirts et livres,
Voilà les choses essentielles,
Pour démontrer savoir vivre.

Pour les femmes, le soir, il faut des jupes,
(Choisissez avec soin.)
Des sarongs peut-être, trois ou quatre robes,
Les sages se débrouillent avec moins.

Ne prenez jamais, (commes idiotes
Au loin pour une seule semaine),
Autant de vêtements qui rempliraient,
La garde-robe de la Reine.

Pour les hommes, des pantalons legers,
Des chemises, ('ne pas repasser'),
Ils n'ont besoin ni de veston,
Ni de cravate. (une chemise est assez.)

La simplicité est à la mode,
Une signe des bonnes manières.
Le plus beau style, dans toutes les îles
Est la tenue de loisirs.

Ces choses suffiront, je pense,
Pour la plupart des pays chauds,
Mais pour les vacances aux Séchelles,
Une autre chose il faut.

Car, dans ces îsles, il pleut beaucoup.
(Le climat est execrable.)
Donc ayez dans une grande valise
Un parapluie formidable.

Mais même en ces îsles pluvieuses,
Enfin brillera le soleil,
Et le ciel, limpide et bleu,
Se fondra dans la baie.

Et quand vous paresserez sur la plage,
Rissolant votre peau si belle,
Votre parapluie deviendra
Une idéale ombrelle.

LINES INSPIRED BY A NOTICE
ON AN AMERICAN GOLF COURSE

'Players entering this area are restricted from loud talking, yelling or otherwise making any noise which can be construed as a noise disturbance ......'

City of Bellevue Parks and Recreation Department

There are things you may not do
On the golf-course at Bellevue.
Check with your attorney when you play.
For, if you should violate
Laws of City or of State,
You'll not be welcome there another day.

Conversation is allowed,
Provided it is not too loud,
When you're on the golf-course at Bellevue.
But you must not ever shout,
Or yell, 'Please take the flag-pole out.'
Or say too loudly, 'What a lovely view.'

How should noises be construed?
Does it matter if they're rude
Or whether someone else is standing near?
When upon the tee you stand,
Is a cry of, 'Well hit!' banned?
Will the Parks Department please make clear?

In what range of decibels
Are loud shouts construed as yells?
Does it depend upon their tone or pitch?
And does it make a difference to
The things that you're allowed to do,
If you are very poor or very rich?

Is it better to permit
Some poor blighter to be hit
On the head or even on the nose,
Or to give a warning shout,
Such as 'Fore' or 'Hey! Look out!'
And risk disturbing somebody's repose.

If, when you're about to play,
Geese upon the fairway stray,
Should you disperse them with a cry of, 'Boo!'
Or silently pick up a rock,
Aim at the centre of the flock,
And see if you can bag a brace or two.

If your ball in someone's garden
Lands, don't shout, 'I beg your pardon.'
Owners will be certain to complain.
They won't give you back your ball,
But will ring the City Hall,
To say they've been disturbed by noise again.

If your partner starts to slice,
You may quietly give advice,
But must be sure that you refrain from yelling.
Householders on nearby plots
May have babies in their cots
And want no noise disturbance near their dwelling.

You may whisper words obscene,
When in one you've reached the green
And miss the putt you needed for an eagle.
But if you should make a noise,
Which might disturb small girls and boys,
There is no doubt that it would be illegal.

On the course you are restricted,
Lest disturbance is inflicted.
Residents don't like disturbing sound.
So, if you're inclined to shout,
And don't want to be thrown out,
Take a vow of silence for the round.

Golf in silence, you will find,
Is beneficial to the mind
And helps you concentrate upon your stroke.
It helps your swing and follow-through,
Your short-play and your putting too,
If you don't have to talk to other folk.

It helps your drives and your approaches,
If no idle talk encroaches,
Nor conversations your attention claim.
So thank-you, City of Bellevue,
For reminding me, as once I knew,
That golf was meant to be a silent game.

Lest readers think that the poet made it up he wants
to make it clear that, apart from correcting what was
obviously a sign-writer's error, he has quoted from the
notice verbatim. The geese on the fairway are not a
figment of his imagination either.

LIGHT AND SHADE

The poems in this section, as the title implies, are a mixture of fairly light-hearted ones interspersed with more serious ones such as 'The Wise Man of Maastricht', 'Soliloquy in a London Phone Box' and 'Party Games'. Most were written in or shortly before 1994, but 'Party Games', 'Tales from Shakespeare' and '*La Jolie Jeune Fille de Bretagne*' are more recent.

SARAH

I thought that first-class crews were getting rarer,
Till someone whispered, 'Have you heard of Sarah?
She gybes a spinnaker in fifteen seconds flat,
But do not shout at her, she won't put up with that.'

I find I have no need to shout, I only applaud 'er,
She knows exactly what to do without an order.
She is intelligent; she is good-looking too.
She is the ideal geriatric helmsman's crew.

I wish she could in Bangor linger longer,
But absence will but make affection stronger.
If she should find another helmsman in some far-off sea,
I hope he shouts at her, so she'll come back to me.

SAUCE FOR THE GOOSE

My crew complains that when we sail,
I always make her pump and bail.
She says that this is most unfair
And that such chores we both should share.

I see that she has got a point,
So will put her nose right out of joint,
By saying, 'Yes, beyond dispute,
We both of us must contribute
To keeping our craft so swift and slim
In the very peak of racing trim.'

So in early March, with gales still howling,
I shall give her a tin of antifouling.

THE WISE MAN OF MAASTRICHT
or
UP YOURS, DELORS!

John Major, *en route* for Maastricht,
Said, 'This treaty has got to be licked.
Jacques Delors' Social Charter
Is a total non-starter.
Its scope I intend to restrict.'

'His plan for a minimum wage,
I shall simply delete from the page.
He can't tell a neighbour
Not to use sweated labour.
It's an absolute bloody outrage.'

'To that damned single-currency scheme,
Obstructive we don't want to seem.
In our time, at our rate,
The Écu could be great.
Until then it remains a pipe dream.'

'The Frogs and the Krauts must be shown
That Great Britain can go it alone.
Eleven can sign
On one dotted line,
But we'll have a line of our own,'

'We shall still be good neighbours, of course,
Though we won't join a peace-keeping force.
Once we've won the election,
We might change direction,
But until then it's, 'Up yours, Delors!"

SOLILOQUY IN A LONDON PHONE-BOX
or BACK TO BASICS

On every wall their cards are there displayed,
But Madam Domina puts others in the Shade.
Her dungeons boast the very latest tackle,
So bondage freaks can choose their favourite shackle.

There's randy, busty, red-head, Kate,
Whose card proclaims she's local, open late,
And there's a Swedish mistress, running a tight ship,
Complete with picture of her with her boots and whip.

Sixteen-year-old submissive schoolgirl thanks
The man who gives her bottom hardest spanks,
And if you should prefer more Latin charms,
Dusky Carlotta waits with open arms.

They all have fancy names, like Karen and Yvette,
Which will not be their real names, you can bet.
Market research has evidently shown,
Men do not fancy Prudence, Patience, Joan.

There is a whole erotic world out there,
Of which the rest of us are only just aware,
A black economy, which government could quickly curb,
But somehow seems reluctant to disturb.

Or do inspectors, clad in dirty macs,
Posing as punters, check their Income Tax
Returns? Or do the Excisemen forsake their tea
To ring them up about their VAT?

Do Advertising Standards men check every card
And when they find exaggeration come down hard?
Do lusty firemen through their windows gape,
To make sure they've a proper fire escape?

No! Rather they turn a suitably blind eye,
Lest some aberrant Minister they spy,
A thing which simply wouldn't do at all,
Now 'Back to Basics' is the rallying call.

SCENES FROM THE CONSULTING-ROOM

The Cardiologist

I'm glad to say your heart was found
To have a nice *staccato* sound,
And, when at rest, *andante* beat
In rhythm which was clear and sweet,
But, during gentle exercise,
Did to a brisk *allegro* rise,
Then with a gradual *rallentando*,
With just a hint of a *glissando*,
Did to its former *tempo* fall,
To cries of *bravo* from us all.

Its strings are taut and full of zing.
It stirs the blood to hear them sing.
It is a heart which knows the score,
And should beat on for some years more.

And, should it fail, do not despair.
I'll fit a temporary spare.
Then scrub it down and rinse it through,
Stick all the loose bits back with glue,
Tune all its strings to concert pitch,
Ensure it has harmonics rich,
Then put it back, (You'll feel no pain.),
To beat *da capo* once again.

And thus you will be *presto* cured.
I take it, Maestro, you're insured?

The Lung Specialist

Your lungs contain the purest air,
Which nowadays is rather rare.
There is so much pollution all around,
That good pure air is very rarely found.
You must live somewhere rural and remote,
Or spend a lot of time on board a sailing boat

West Kirby Promenade you say?
Ah! Now I understand.
I wondered why your bronchial tubes
Were full of salt and sand.

The Haematologist

I've had a chance to take a careful look
At that small sample of your blood I took,
I spread it out quite thinly on a slide
And, looking through my microscope, espied
Corpuscles of each blood-group in the text-books listed
And several more I didn't know existed.

Into accepted theory this cannot be fitted.
Only one blood-group for each person is permitted.
It's very strange; a second opinion I must seek.
To put it bluntly, sir, you are a freak,
Or bloody odd (to use the medical vernacular).
What did you say your name was, sir?

Count Dracula?

A Liver Complaint

A complaint about your liver?
Is that what I heard you say
No other customer complained
And we sell a lot each day.

It comes from the nearest abattoir.
We collect it fresh from there.
Are you sure you cooked it properly?
You should not eat liver rare.

Has there been some confusion?
My hearing's rather poor.
This is the butcher's, Madam.
The doctor's is next door.

The Hand Surgeon

Your finger's bent, you say,
And in your glove won't fit.
It's not a rare condition, sir,
And there's a cure for it.

I'll simply cut the finger off;
I will not hesitate.
And so as not to waste your time,
I'll do it while you wait.

Quick! Nurse! He's turning pale.
He's fainted. Bring him round.
I can't abide the sight of patients
Prone upon the ground.

Oh what a fuss! I'm quite upset.
God help us! Heavens above!
And all because I said I'd cut
The finger off his glove.

TALES FROM SHAKESPEARE

Romeo and Juliet

Brave Romeo fell in love with beautiful Juliet,
But he was a Montague and she was a Capulet.
Enmity between their families had long ago been sworn,
And they were still at daggers drawn,
So that tragedy was certain to ensue
From any relationship between the star-crossed two.

King Lear

King Lear failed to make it clear,
That although he had delegated
Day-to-day administration,
He was still the monarch of the nation
And expected a respectful salutation.

So it drove him mad,
When his two dreadful daughters,
Instead of calling him, 'Your Majesty',
Insisted on calling him, 'Dad'.

Too late he recovered his sanity,
And, with Cordelia's body in his arms,
Saw the result of his stupidity and vanity.

A Midsummer-Night's Dream

When Bottom found that he'd been 'translated',
He thought at first that he was ill-fated.
But he didn't mind having an ass's head,
When he found himself in Titania's bed,
Even though he thought it was a bit obscene,
For an Ass to make love to a Fairy Queen.
He didn't realise that he owed his luck
To the efforts of Oberon's attendant, Puck.

Othello, The Moor of Venice

Othello was a loyal servant of the Venetian state,
And as a general he was first rate,
But the trust he reposed in Iago, his wily subordinate,
Was mis-placed and inordinate.
He was tricked by Iago into killing his innocent wife,
And, on learning the truth, he took his own life.

Julius Caesar

For Caesar, J,
The Ides of March was an unlucky day.
But he had a good funeral accolade,
Which his friend, Antony, M, obligingly made.

Mark Antony

Mark Antony, while disclaiming any rhetorical skill,
Mounted the rostrum on the Capitoline Hill,
To portray his avaricious friend, Julius Caesar,
As really a rather benevolent old geezer.
Saying that thrice he had presented him a kingly crown,
And Caesar thrice had turned the offer down.

Hamlet

Prince Hamlet couldn't make up his mind,
Because his long-term objectives were too ill-defined.

If he had lived a century or two later,
An intensive course of psychoanalysis
Might have helped to overcome his mental paralysis,
Except that he wouldn't have been able to avoid
Having to decide whether to consult
Karl Jüng or Sigmund Freud.

Macbeth

That brave Scottish soldier, Macbeth,
Didn't fear a violent death,
Because an apparition had sworn
That he couldn't be harmed
By one of woman born.
So he went on strutting his stuff,
Forgetting that he had also been told
To beware Macduff.

Banquo

Banquo couldn't come to Macbeth's feast,
Because he was deceased.
But so as not to disappoint his host,
He sent his ghost,
Who, entering just in time to hear grace read,
Sat down, invisible to other guests, at table's head.

Only Macbeth could see him and, turning pale,
With foaming mouth began to rant and rail,
Till Lady Macbeth, who'd had a nasty fright,
Thought it was time to bid the guests 'good night!'
And they, though knowing that outside a gale was blowing,
Stood not upon the order of their going.

Lady Macbeth

Lady Macbeth made a terrible scene,
Because she couldn't wash
Her bloody hands clean.
Perhaps the outcome
Would have been less diabolic,
If she had known about carbolic.

THE PROFESSIONALS

When Jack and Jill were married,
Their friends were very glad.
He was a merchant banker;
She had a wealthy dad.
The omens seemed set fair for them;
They were toasted in champagne.
They had their honeymoon in France,
Then a holiday in Spain.

But when they both came back again,
Their friends at once perceived
That he was frowning all the time
And she seemed sorely grieved.
It took some time before they found
What had blighted married bliss,
But when the tale at last emerged,
It was, quite simply, this.

They were quite incompatible
And in a sorry plight.
Jack only made love by the light of dawn,
Jill only late at night.
Their friends all came to comfort them,
And said, 'Please take advice'
They replied, 'We know we ought to,
But it doesn't seem quite nice.'

But soon they saw that they had no choice
But to swallow down their pride,
And so, for Marriage Guidance,
They first of all applied.
The Counsellor listened carefully,
Then sadly shook his head,
'I'm not allowed to talk about
Things that go on in bed.'

'I can talk about togetherness,
And empathy and such,
But I'm a bachelor myself
And have never made love much.
You really need sex therapy,
Or possibly a shrink.
I'm sorry to sound unhelpful,
But that is what I think.'

The Therapist was busy,
And after a long wait,
Said, 'Jack, come back without your wife.
I think we could relate.'
Jack declined her invitation;
He was not that way inclined,
And guessed the sort of relationship,
Which she had got in mind.

They went to a psychiatrist,
Who said, 'You're out of synch;
An engineer is what you need
And not a hard-worked shrink.
But still they went to other shrinks;
They went to four that day,
But whatever one of them advised,
The next said, 'No! No Way!'

They read the Kama Sutra,
Which is full of sayings wise.
They learnt some new positions,
But could still not synchronise.
They were really in the dumps by then
And thought that the only course
Was either an annulment,
Or else a quick divorce.

But, quite by chance, they met that day,
When they thought their marriage wrecked,
An interior designer
And a landscape architect.
They told them of their problems
And their constant arguments.
They replied, 'We'll come round straight away
And take some measurements'

'We think that the solution
Is really pretty clear.
It needs a little detailed work;
We'll soon be in top gear.'
The next day they rang up to say,
'We've finalized our plan
And ordered the equipment
And will bring it in our van.'
'For Jack we've heavy curtains,

To shut out all the light.
He must draw them in the morning,
So Jill will think it's night.
For Jill we've got some floodlights,
To set up on your lawn.
She must switch them on at midnight,
To make Jack think it's dawn.'

'The curtains will be interlined,
With pelmets at their head,
Electrically controlled of course,
With a switch beside Jack's bed.
The floodlights will be landscaped in,
With cables underground,
Concealed behind a shrubbery,
Which we will plant around.'

It was a most ingenious plan;
That cannot be denied.
They made love twice on every night
And were doubly satisfied.
Their children are grown up by now
And deserving of respect,
An interior designer
And a landscape architect.

Envoi:

So waste no time on counsellors;
Never go near a shrink;
Ignore the wiles of therapists;
They are not what people think

The experts that you should consult
On problems to do with sex
Are interior designers
And landscape architects.

So if you satisfaction seek,
There is no career that's finer
Than that of a landscape architect
Or interior designer.

AUNT AGONY REPLIES

Jealousy

You have a rival, so you say,
He knew her long before your wedding day,
And though she was a bridesmaid when you wed,
You're certain that they used to share a bed.
You're green with jealousy, you write,
And say you caught him phoning her last night.
The day before, you say, he hugged and kissed her.
Come off it, dear. You know she's his twin sister.

Obsessions

He has six Flying Scots, you say, that sounds obsessive
And fifteen signal boxes is a bit excessive.
You say more rolling stock came yesterday,
And there's another twenty feet of track to lay.
You'll have to build a home extension, dear,
So you can keep the lounge and hallway clear.
If not you will be short of space indeed,
When your Malayan gibbons start to breed.

Infidelity

You say he makes love twenty times a week
And that you think he does it out of pique.
That is a lot of times of course,
But hardly grounds for separation or divorce.

I've turned the page. Ah! Now I catch your drift,
You have the makings of a serious rift.
You say, my dear, he is not being true,
And does it when he's not in bed with you.
This is a situation up with which you should not put.
Give him and inch and he will take a foot.
Go find a lover, That's what I enjoin,
And pay your husband swiftly back in his own coin.

CEASEFIRE

A ceasefire is a welcome thing, or so it seems to me,
Though the Reverend Ian Paisley appears to disagree.

So I will drink a toast to peace, but will not make too merry,
Till I see Paisley, Ian, shake hands with Adams, Gerry.

For nothing is impossible to truly gifted men.
We've seen De Klerk, F.W., embrace Mandela, N.

And as another instance of what I'm getting at,
We've seen Yitszhak Rabin sit down with Yassir Arafat.

If I had prophesied all this, you'd have said 'Don't be absurd.'
But now we've seen two miracles, might we not see a third?

So I will not break out my flags, nor raise my joyful paean,
Till I see Adams, Gerry, shake hands with Paisley, Ian.

PEACE PROCESS

I am an English Liberal,
Though less naïve than some;
Five minutes of Gerry Adams
Has me beating the Orange drum.

But Unionist intransigence
I cannot long sustain;
Five minutes of Ian Paisley
Has me cheering for Sinn Fein.

The attitude of each of them
In my breast such ire arouses,
That I'm tempted to say, with Shakespeare,
'A plague on both your houses!

But instead, I will encourage them
To cut the word-war short;
The one that first shuts up, for good,
Shall have my full support.

PARTY GAMES

A party has but one intent
And but one common cause.
It wants to be the Government
And frame the Nation's laws.
Its members won't all think the same,
But argument is forbidden,
For it's part of the party political game
To keep disagreement hidden.

No party's members all agree,
But must pretend they do,
For speech in Parliament is not free,
Whether you're red or blue.
Each party likes to mock with glee
The other's public schism,
While pretending that it is totally free
From deviationism.

A backbencher, or party hack,
As he's disrespectfully known,
Is never allowed to stray from the track
Or express a view of his own.
For if he wants to climb the tree,
(That is, obtain promotion),
He has to vote as the whips decree
On every conceivable motion.

If he plans to rebel and his bluff is called
And the whip is then withdrawn.
Members would not be too appalled,
If he were shot at dawn.
For it simply isn't done to show
Such public disaffection,
Especially as you never know
When there might be a snap election.

If a minister's caught with his trousers down
On some sordid assignation,
The whips will give him a dressing-down
And require his resignation.

No sympathy will he be shown;
The PM will withdraw support.
He's broken the oldest commandment known,
Namely, 'Thou shalt not be caught.'

He'll lose his chance of becoming a peer;
Disgrace will be his fate.
He'll have to start a new career
And rehabilitate.
But to help him overcome his shame,
There are some jobs where he can go,
Such as chairing a TV panel game
Or even a minor quango.

But if a minister's just obtuse
And so lacking in all ability,
That his party decides that he's no use
And a serious liability.
When Nemesis finally catches up
And he leaves the Government ranks,
There'll be headhunters waiting to sign him up
For the boards of merchant banks.

For even a junior minister (ex)
Looks good on the letter-head,
Provided he's stuck to conventional sex
And kept out of his secretary's bed.
For if he knows the Whitehall way
And has contacts with whom to chat
He is probably worth what the bankers pay,
Though he may be a stupid prat.

I hope, when you read this, you'll not think
That I don't like politicians.
For I know that they have their role to play,
Just like dentists or dieticians.
But my underlying argument,
The conclusion at which I aim,
Is that bad as is any Government,
The next will be just the same.

LA JOLIE JEUNE FILLE DE BRETAGNE
(A Limerick in Six Versions)

Une Jolie Jeune Fille de Bretagne
Liked to streak when the weather was fine.
She would boast, 'It's not rude
To sprint in the nude,
When you have a nice figure like mine.'

Une Jolie Jeune Fille de Bretagne
Liked to streak when the weather was fine.
When *gendarmes* gave chase,
They could not stand the pace,
And collapsed on the finishing line.

Une Jolie Jeune Fille de Bretagne
Liked to streak when the weather was fine.
When a *gendarme* pursued,
She used language quite lewd
And words I'd not care to define.

Une Jolie Jeune Fille de Bretagne
Liked to streak when the weather was fine.
Gendarmes tried to arrest her,
But dared not molest her,
So imposed a fixed penalty fine.

Une Jolie Jeune Fille de Bretagne
Liked to streak when the weather was fine.
Crowds came out to cheer
And offered her beer.
Elle dit, 'Merci, je préfère Champagne.'

Une Jolie Jeune Fille de Bretagne
Liked to streak when the weather was fine.
Dit un gendarme, 'Mam'selle,
Vous êtes vraiment très belle,
Shall we make love at your place or mine?'

THE BORGIA FAMILY

Alexander, the Borgia Pope,
Whose family were quite beyond hope,
When asked why on earth
He'd not hanged them at birth,
Said, 'I tried but they'd hidden the rope.'

His wife was a beauty, it's said,
And made Alexander see red,
By preferring the charms
Of her fancy boy's arms
To those of the marital bed.

Caesar, their horrible son,
Had a pretty odd notion of fun,
For he, for his joys,
Preferred goats to small boys,
And rode them all night one by one.

Their daughter was the Lady Lucrezia.
You'd find if she said, 'Come and eat dear.'
She had poisoned your wine,
Ere you sat down to dine,
And would sprinkle ground glass on your pizza.

The Pope got fed up with his wife,
And her lewd and adulterous life.
So with poison well tried,
Namely pure cyanide,
Put an end to his trouble and strife.

Caesar, a mile in the rear,
Encouraged his troops, 'Never fear!'
But one day a stray shot
Pierced an unarmoured spot,
And St.Peter's rang out a great cheer.

Lady L blended poisons with zest,
Her technology always the best.
Till a servant, from spite,
Dressed her salad one night,
With arsenic meant for a guest.

And so Alexander survived,
Of all of his family deprived.
He sat back on his throne,
And said, 'Good! I'm alone.
I feel that I've really arrived.'

LA FAMIGLIA BORGIA

Allessandro, il papa orribile,
La famiglia era irrimediabile,
Quando chiesto, 'A nato,
Perché non impiccato?'
Di 'l'ho tento ma era impossibile.'

La moglie era bella da nato,
E Allessandro era molto irato.
Giaceva nonostante,
Nel letto del amante,
E il suo era abbandonato.

Cesàr, loro figlio, era male.
Suo gusto era eccezionale.
Preferiava I capretti,
Per piacer' ai ragazzetti,
E montava nel palazzo papale.

Loro figlia, la Signora Lucrezia,
Quand l'invito in sua fortezza,
A avvelenato il suo vino,
Prima di sedersi al tavolino,
E a spolverizzato vetro molinato sulla pizza.

Il Papa, la pazienza rotta,
Per la moglie e sua condotta.
Con veleno sicuro.
Cioè cianuro puro,
Finì il disturbo e la lotta.

Cesàr, da un chilometro,
Incorragia le sue truppe indietro.
Ma l'abbattuto,
Un missile perduto,
E si suona la campana di San Pietro.

Mascolava Lucrezia con cura,
La tecnica sempre sicura,
Finchè servo irato,
Condimento l'ha dato,
Con arsenico nella verdura.

Allessandro era così lasciato,
La famiglia morta, suo fato.
Insediato sul trono,
Di, 'solo! È Buono.
Mi sento veramente arrivato.'

A NIGHT AT THE OPERA

The poem in this section summarizes the plot of a grand opera in easily memorizable verse which can be recited *sotto voce* during the performance, making surtitles and other distracting aids to comprehension, and, on occasion, even the performance itself, totally superfluous.

LA CLEMENZA DI TITO

Composed in 1791 by Wolfgang Amadeus Mozart

Libretto by Caterina Mazzolà

Based on a text by Pietro Metastasio

DRAMATIS PERSONAE

TITO/TITUS
(Tenor)

Emperor of Rome 79-81 AD
Son of Vespasian, Emperor of Rome 69-79 AD

VITELLIA
(Soprano)

Daughter of Vitellius, Emperor of Rome 69 AD
reputedly murdered on the orders of Vespasian

SESTO/SEXTUS
(Soprano or Mezzo-Soprano)

in love with Vitellia

SERVILIA
(Soprano)

Sister of Sesto, in love with Annio

ANNIO/ANNIUS
(Soprano or Mezzo-Soprano)

a friend of Sesto, in love with Servilia

PUBLIO/PUBLIUS
(Bass)

Commander of the Imperial Guard

NOTES

The action takes place in Rome in 80 AD at about the time of the eruption of Vesuvius which destroyed Pompeii and Herculaneum. The Senate had voted funds for a temple to be dedicated to Titus and his decision to scale down the project and apply the funds saved to the relief of victims of the eruption is used as one of several examples of his generosity.

Lentulus, a principal accomplice in the conspiracy which Sextus leads, is not included in the *Dramatis Personae* and the *libretto* suggests that his accidental wounding by Sextus takes place off stage, but in some productions it takes place on stage.

Titus, the Emperor gentle,
Had a girl-friend of race oriental.
She said, 'Not till we're wed,
Will I come to your bed.
We Hebrews are not sentimental.'

The Senate, the Emperor's court,
Said, 'You must have a Roman consort.
Berenice's bad news;
She must take a long cruise.
You may bid her farewell at the port.'

He agreed, though with tears his eyes ran.
Publius said, 'That's the spirit, old man.
Now we've got some good news
And would welcome your views
On the new city temple we plan.'

'Here's some gold from the latest campaign,
Sufficient to build and maintain
An imposing erection
Of noble perfection.
A statue of you 'twill contain.'

''Twill portray, with appropriate force,
You astride your most fearsome war-horse.
And the whole population
Of our Roman nation
Will pray to you daily of course.'

Publius paused, the reply to await.
Titus said, 'Your proposal's just great,
But I can't be a God,
Till I'm under the sod,
And I'd rather be living than late.'

'So the details I'd like to adjust,
And I know you'll agree, as you must,
So, a temple quite small,
By the old city hall,
And, instead of a statue, a bust.'

'With the money thus saved, here's my brief,
For a fund for disaster relief,
To house, clothe and feed
Refugees when in need,
And I'll be the Patron-in-Chief.'

To throng him the populace tried,
And 'Glory to Titus!' they cried,
'What a far-sighted plan!
What a generous man!'
'It's my pleasure.' He quietly replied.

Next, a Roman wife he had to find,
And he'd heard that Servilia was kind.
When she said, 'I'm engaged.'
He was (mildly) enraged,
But thanked her for speaking her mind.

'Please tell me your chosen one's name.'
'He's a Roman of family and fame.
It is Annius, my lord,
Whom I've always adored,
And his feelings for me are the same.'

'Then you have my permission to wed.'
The benevolent Emperor said.
'For Annius is loyal
To the family royal,
Which is more than can sometimes be said.'

'And as for a marriage for me,
I would frankly much rather be free,
But the Senate insist
I work through their short list,
So Vitellia's the next I must see.'

'She knows Sextus, your brother, they say,
And he's up at her villa each day.
She can't still be mad
That dad murdered her dad,
So I'll make her my Empress today.'

'I'll send Publius to bring her to court,
With a suitably regal escort.
He can wait while she presses
A skirt and some dresses.
I would not want her hurriedly brought.'

In the meantime, young Sextus, un-knowing,
With his love for Vitellia glowing,
Had nailed up at last
His flag to the mast
And set a rebellion going.

When he heard about Publius' news,
Which quite altered Vitellia's views,
He could not countermand
The revolt he had planned,
For he'd lit the Capitoline fuse.

So he hurried to join his friends bold,
And for reasons that soon will be told,
The one blow that he struck,
By a piece of bad luck,
Knocked his pal, poor old Lentulus, cold.

For it seems that old Lent and his guys
Had decided to put on disguise.
As the Emperor dressed,
Lent's disguise was the best,
But Sextus he'd failed to put wise.

So when Sextus had clobbered his friend,
The imperial cloak he did rend.
'Take that, Titus.' he said,
As he really saw red,
'Your villainy's now at an end.'

But soon he was full of remorse,
And said as he fled on his horse,
'Look what I've done now,
For that stupid old cow!
I'll be thrown to the lions of course.'

The remaining insurgents grew pale.
Their revolt was now certain to fail.
Though they fought them quite hard,
The Imperial Guard
Soon had them locked up in the jail.

A warrant for Sextus' arrest
Was issued at Titus' behest.
High and low he was sought
And was pretty soon caught
And locked up in jail with the rest.

Annius heard pretty soon of the rap,
And exclaimed in a terrible flap,
'This I cannot believe;
I will seek a reprieve;
Sextus isn't that sort of a chap.'

'When Sextus was brought to the court,
He said, 'Let the proceedings be short.
I admit my transgression
And will sign a confession.'
'I'll be thrown to the lions.' he thought.

But to his surprise they said, 'Steady!
The Emperor isn't quite ready.
He'd quite like to know
Why you hated him so,
But he's stayed execution already.'

They brought Titus in on his throne
And he said , 'Now please leave us alone.'
He took Sextus' hand
As he knelt in the sand,
And spoke in the kindliest tone.

'Vitellia and I've had a chat
And now I'm quite satisfied that
'Twas her venom and spite
That made you uptight,
And I can't really blame you for that.'

'So, I'll grant you a pardon,' he said,
'On condition that you and she wed.
So trouble and strife,
For the rest of your life,
Will pursue you all day and in bed.'

'As for me, I shall single remain.
I find courtship too much of a strain.
My brother, Domitian,
Can have my position,
So it stays in the Flavian line.'

'A pardon I'm offering, too,
To the rest of your treacherous crew.
Though Rome's queued half the night
For seats for the fight,
And the lions are the best in the zoo.'

'So now to the circus I'll go,
To tell them I've cancelled the show.
The crowd's pretty large
And they'll jostle and barge,
For they're not going to like it, I know.'

At the circus he mounted the stand,
In his crown and his toga so grand,
'Dear Romans,' he called,
'Please don't be appalled,
I've forgiven the treacherous band.'

'They have shown quite disgraceful bad form,
But deserve one more chance to reform.
I'll refund what you've paid,
And while lions parade,
The band of the Guards will perform.'

At first they could hardly believe
That the villains had gained a reprieve.
There were cries of, 'Bad show!
You can't let them go.
They set out to murder and thieve.'

But soon wiser counsel prevailed,
And Titus' mercy they hailed.
'He is such a good chap,
That he fears no mishap.
That is why the conspiracy failed.'

At that all the senators stood,
To sing praise to their Emperor good.
Those of evil intent
Vowed that they would repent,
So the opera could end as it should.

THE WELSH CONNECTION

The poems in this section were written in or shortly before 1994. 'The Ladies of Wales' and 'More About the Ladies of Wales' are frolics which revel in the wonderfully mellifluous quality of the Welsh language although the need to find a rhyme has meant that some of the places mentioned are in England. Readers who think that some of the verses are too risqué may skip them.

'Trilogy on a Welsh Road Sign' needs no explanation.

THE LADIES OF WALES

A housewife from near Aberdaron
Had mistakenly thought she was barren,
So when quintuplets came,
She was stuck for a name,
And decided to call them all Sharon.

An ambitious young woman from Barry
Said, 'The man that I'm going to marry
Will be a duke's heir,
Or a millionaire,
And not any Tom, Dick or Harry.'

A sixteen-year-old from Caergwrle
Went to bed and complained she felt poorly.
'I feel funny inside.
Am I pregnant?' she cried.
Her mother said, 'Not again, surely?'

Said a sex-starved old maid from Deganwy,
When she first went to bed with a man, 'We
Musn't get caught,
But it's marvellous sport.
Let us meet again soon dear. When can we?'

A waitress from Eglwys Bach
Was made to get up with the lark.
She laid tables all day,
But so poor was the pay,
She earned more getting laid after dark.

An extravagant heiress from Flint
Spent all she was left, without stint.
Friends, being more wise,
Told her, 'Economise'.
But she didn't, and finished up skint.

The Ladies of Wales

A prolific young girl from Gaerwen
Had six children, all under ten.
When asked, 'Can you cope?'
She replied, 'Not a hope,
If their dads didn't help now and then.'

A young PE teacher from Holywell
Told her pupils that sex was a folly. Well,
The Governors heard
And said, 'That is absurd.'
She was sacked, though she played hockey jolly well.

A boastful young climber on Idwal,
Near the top said, 'I think that I did well.'
But forgot her belays
And, still full of self-praise,
At the bottom announced that she slid well.

A lazy young girl from Kidwelly
Spent the whole of one week watching telly.
She did without nosh,
Didn't bother to wash,
And finished up hungry and smelly.

A woman from Llanfair PG
Invited her boy friend to tea.
With cries of delight,
They made love half the night,
Sustained by large cups of PG.

A middle-aged granny from Mold
Said, 'I simply can't face growing old.
Cosmetics and creams
Can't restore faded dreams,
But a good lover helps, so I'm told.'

A dominant lady from Neath
Got the femininist bit 'tween her teeth.
She said, 'When I make love,
I must be above
The inferior sex underneath.

A choir-girl, who came from Oswestry,
Was proud of her wealthy ancestry,
But her grandfather still
Cut her out of his will,
For seducing a priest in the vestry.

A promiscuous girl from Pendine
Had the men queueing up in a line.
There was no need for gin,
To tempt her to sin.
She would come across nicely on wine.

At Christmas, a girl from Queensferry
Stood under the mistletoe berry.
To the first man who kissed her,
She said, 'I'm your sister.
You must be a little too merry.'

An unscrupulous typist from Rhaiadr
Seduced each employer who hired 'er,
Then threatened to tell,
If they didn't pay well,
And took them to court if they fired 'er.

A stripper from Sarn bet a fiver,
She could emulate Lady Godiva.
Riding round in the buff
In mid-winter is tough.
She froze and they couldn't revive 'er.

The Ladies of Wales

A gluttonous girl from Treorchy
Grew so fat that her friends called her, 'Porky'.
So to keep them all quiet,
She went on a diet,
And now she is tall, thin and gawky.

An unfortunate woman from Usk
Had a tooth like an elephant's tusk.
Her appearance caused cries
Of alarm and surprise,
So she only went out after dusk.

A popular call-girl from Valley
Plied her trade from a cosy beach-chalet.
Aircraftmen from the camp
Queued beneath her red lamp,
And the lucky ones stayed till reveille.

A mischievous woman from Wrexham
Hated men and decided to vex 'em.
With a promise to wed,
She would lure them to bed,
Then pull out a knife and unsex 'em.

A woman from Ysbyty Ifan,
Was jilted and swore to get even.
To her rival she said,
'He is useless in bed.
Good riddance! You won't find me grievin.'

An erotic skin-diver from Zeal
Said, 'I've been making love with an eel.
He's electric and so
He emits a bright glow
And has a nice tingling feel.'

TRILOGY ON A WELSH ROAD SIGN

Canto One

Aber was once a village pretty,
'Twixt Llanfairfechan and Bangor city.
Above it, down their rocky walls,
Thundered (on rainy days) the Aber Falls

As Aber it was always known to me,
Since childhood holidays beside the sea.
Sprawling beside the old A55,
It was a village quiet, but still alive.

Now they have built a by-pass, arrow straight,
To speed the traffic to and from the Menai Strait.
The drivers now are scarcely conscious that,
They've flashed past Aber in ten seconds flat.

'Does Aber still exist?' I ask, the question begging,
The signposts all now read, 'Abergwyngregyn'.
Aber is dead. No by-pass quenched its ancient flames,
But this mad passion for inventing new Welsh names

Aber, I fear, is written out of history.
But what about the Aber Falls? Now there's a mystery.
When next I walk up to those rocky walls,
Will rustic signs read 'Abergwyngregyn Falls'?

Canto Two

When the grand-children cluster round my knee,
To hear their bed-time stories after tea,
To hear my tales of times now long-since past,
Before all towns and villages had been by-passed,
Will they believe, or simply be appalled,
That Abergwyngregyn was once Aber Called?

Will they believe that where the water crashes,
Before dispersing in a thousand splashes,
Thundering down between the rocky walls,
(on rainy days) was once the Aber Falls?
Will they believe such tales from memory's dusty locker?
Or call, 'Come quickly Granny, Grandpa's off his rocker.'

Canto three

A tourist, when visiting Aber,
Complained that the falls didn't grab 'er.
'When it's rained for some days,
They may make good displays.
On a dry day they couldn't be drabber.'

'There is not' she said, dipping a leg in,
'Enough water to boil a small egg in.'
Did I say it was Aber,
Whose falls didn't grab 'er?
My mistake, I meant Abergwyngregyn.

MORE ABOUT THE LADIES OF WALES
(And Introductions to Some New Ones)

A woman from Abertillery
Once got into bed with a fairy.
The result of this deed
Was, of course, a cross-breed,
Half mortal and Welsh and half fairy.

You remember the woman from Barry,
Who said a duke's heir she would marry?
I am sad to relate
That none rose to her bait.
She still works in the same cash-and-carry.

You remember the girl from Caergwrle?
She had worried her mum prematurely.
For she had not conceived
And was greatly relieved
To discover she was merely poorly.

You recall the old maid from Deganwy,
Who at last went to bed with a man? I
Hear she's so sprightly,
She makes love twice nightly,
And still says, 'Once more dear, when can we?'

Said a witty young woman from Ewloe,
Whose lover had called her a fool, 'Oh
My dear, you should know,
My IQ is not low
Unlike yours, which is certainly too low.'

You remember the heiress from Flint,
Who squandered and finished up skint?
She gave it a whirl
As a kissogram girl,
And now she is making a mint.

More about the ladies of Wales

You remember the girl from Gaerwen,
Who had six children, all under ten?
If there'd been fourteen more,
She'd have had a round score
And needed a larger play pen.

You remember the teacher from Holywell,
Who was sacked on account of her folly? Well
She damages sought
And obtained from the court,
And now she looks after her lolly well.

You remember the climber who slid well,
Having boastfully claimed that she did well?
She fell once again
And left a red stain
Of blood on the slabs of Cwm Idwal.

You remember the girl from Kidwelly,
Who finished up hungry and smelly?
She's still idle as sin,
But not quite so thin,
As she eats while she's watching the telly.

A housewife took a coach to Llandudno,
She was passionate in all that she did. No
Man she would spare.
She'd cry, 'Kiss me right there,
But don't my old man and kid know.'

You remember the granny from Mold,
Who could simply not face growing old?
A good lover she found,
But he's now underground.
She worked him to death, so I'm told.

More about the ladies of Wales

You remember the lady from Neath
Who made love with the man underneath?
When she lay on his chest,
One poor chap was compressed,
But she made him a very nice wreath.

You recall the choir-girl from Oswestry,
Whose good reputation went west? Re'
Formed she is not
And she still spends a lot
Of her time with the priest in the vestry

You remember the girl from Pendine,
Who would come across nicely on wine?
Even one glass of whisky
Would make her more frisky
And she'd dance in the nude after nine.

You remember the girl from Queensferry,
Who was kissed 'neath the mistletoe berry?
The same time next year,
She was still kissing there.
'Are you happy?' I asked. She said, 'Very!'

A naturist, bathing at Rhyl,
Took off all her clothes for a thrill.
A beach-guard drew near,
Said, 'You can't do that here.'
And took her behind a sand-hill.

You remember the stripper who tried,
Like Lady Godiva to ride?
From exposure to snow,
She died as you know,
But in Sarn she's remembered with pride.

More about the ladies of Wales

You remember the girl from Treorchy,
Whose diet made her tall, thin and gawky?
Her friends told her that,
Men prefer women fat,
So now, once again, she's called 'Porky'.

In Uwchmynnydd a lady once dwelt,
Who could never recall how 'twas spelt.
'It begins with a 'U',
There's a 'Y' perhaps two.'
She said, with frustration heartfelt.

You remember the call-girl from Valley,
Who worked from last post to reveille?
Up market she's moved
And her image improved.
Even officers come to her chalet.

You remember the woman from Wrexham,
Who took men to bed to unsex 'em?
She discovered too late
That, when you castrate
Men, it doesn't improve them it wrecks 'em.

A lady from old Ynys Môn
Was continually leading men on.
They swarmed round her like flies,
Then got a surprise,
When she said, 'I can't stand you. Begone!'

You remember the diver from Zeal,
Who made love with a twenty volt eel.
With his battery flat,
There was no more of that,
So she cooked him to make a square meal.

ANOTHER NIGHT AT THE OPERA

The poem in this section summarizes the plot of a grand opera in easily memorizable verse which can be recited *sotto voce* during the performance, making surtitles and other distracting aids to comprehension, and, on occasion, even the performance itself, totally superfluous.

LUCIA DI LAMMERMOOR

Composed in 1835 by Gaetano Donizetti

Libretto by Salvatore Cammarano

Based on Sir Walter Scott's novel, 'The Bride of Lammermoor'

DRAMATIS PERSONAE

ENRICO/HENRY, LORD ASHTON
(Baritone)

Usurping Laird of Ravenswood

LUCIA/LUCY ASHTON
(Soprano)

Enrico's Sister

EDGARDO/EDGAR
(Tenor)

Rightful Heir to Ravenswood

ARTURO/ARTHUR, LORD BUCKLAW
(Tenor)

RAIMONDO/RAYMOND
(Bass)

Enrico's Chaplain and *Lucia*'s Tutor

ALISA/ALICE
(Mezzo-Soprano)

Lucia's Lady's Maid and Companion

NORMANNO/NORMAN
(Tenor)

Enrico's Head Huntsman

Programme Notes

The story of this opera,
Though altered quite a lot,
Is based upon a novel
By the great Sir Walter Scott.

The tale unfolds in Scotland,
In the lonely Lammermuirs,
In a rather run-down castle,
Close by the North Sea's shores.

There's been some sort of *coup d'etat*,
It isn't quite clear what.
Operatic grasp of politics
Is never all that hot.

Enrico, Laird of Ravenswood,
Was on the losing side,
And this has been serious blow
To his wealth and family pride.

He has one ace left in his hand,
An extremely pretty sister,
Lucia, a maid so very fair
No suitor could resist her.

She's the asset in his balance sheet,
Which he must realize,
And he's found a well-heeled nobleman,
Who will pay for such a prize.

Arturo, Laird of Bucklaw,
Owns lands and loads of cash,
But though he's young he's rather wet
And doesn't cut a dash.

This, we will see, is the one slight snag
In *Enrico*'s rescue plan.
He fears *Lucia* won't play ball,
For she loves another man.

He's called *Edgardo* and, what's more,
He is the rightful heir
To the broad estates of Ravenswood,
With their woods and pastures fair.

Enrico killed *Edgardo*'s dad,
When *Edgardo* was a child,
And, now *Edgardo*'s come of age,
A claim in tort he's filed.

And if due legal process
Will not enforce his claim,
He's sworn that with his good sharp sword
He'll win it just the same.

He's sworn he'll run *Enrico* through
And, like a shish kebab,
Lay the false Laird of Ravenswood
On a mortuary slab.

You'll agree, having heard the background,
That you could not expect
Enrico to want *Edgardo*
As his brother-in-law elect.

Act I, Scene 1

When first the curtain rises,
Enrico's men are here,
Singing a pre-dawn chorus,
Whose words are not too clear.

Enrico doesn't mean to let
Edgardo rub him out,
So he's organized a thorough search
Of the country round about.

Normanno, *Enrico*'s huntsman,
Tells the searchers where to go,
Then says, 'A word, *Enrico*, please,
There are things you ought to know.'

- 89 -

'*Lucia* is a winsome lass
And knows the facts of life.
She sees *Edgardo* frequently
and rumour has been rife.'

'I was near when he first met her,
Being chased by a maddened bull.
He saved her life with a single shot,
Which gave it a bellyful.'

'It's said he meets her every morn
In a garden on your lands
And I'm prepared to wager
That they don't just hold hands.'

Raimondo, the unctuous chaplain,
At first takes *Lucia*'s side,
And says, 'This is speculation,
Some proof must be supplied.'

'I know she spurns *Arturo*,
And says he has bad breath,
But I think it's because she's still upset
By her mother's recent death.'

'I think she needs a bit more time
And must be strung along.'
(He's realized that, if she doesn't wed,
His employment won't last long.)

But *Enrico*'s badly worried
By what *Normanno* said
And direful possibilities
Keep turning in his head.

'The searchers then return in haste,
To deliver their report.
They are sure they've seen *Edgardo*
Ride through the Wolf's Crag Court.

'He can't escape us now.' They cry
And raise a joyful shout,
'We'll wait until it's daybreak
And then we'll seek him out.'

'We'll capture him alive for you,
So you can take his head.
Or we can save you trouble,
By capturing him dead.'

This was an idle boast of theirs,
As we shall shortly see,
For *Edgardo* evaded capture,
And soon put out to sea.

Act I, Scene 2

The scene is in a garden,
With a fountain in the shade,
And *Lucia* enters nervously,
With *Alisa*, her lady's maid.

It will not take you long to guess,
It's *Edgardo* for whom they're waiting,
And soon you'll see that *Normanno*
Was not exaggerating.

Lucia tells *Alisa*,
As they wait with baited breath,
How a jealous heir of Ravenswood
Once stabbed a girl to death.

He threw her body in the well,
Which polluted it quite badly,
And her ghost still haunts the garden
And sings there rather sadly.

Lucia had once seen her there,
On a misty moonless night,
But when she tried to talk to her
She disappeared from sight.

'*Lucia*,' said *Alisa*,
'This is an omen clear,
That your love for brave *Edgardo*
Will lead you to your bier.'

'You'll have to give him up, *Lucia*,
As your brother thinks is fit,
And marry that wimp, *Arturo*,
Although he is a twit.'

Lucia will not listen
And says, 'Avaunt! Begone!
Edgardo is the only man
Who has ever turned me on.'

At this, *Edgardo* enters,
And says, 'I'm off to France,
Where I have several wealthy friends,
Who can give me an advance.'

'But, before I catch the ferry,
I'd like to do a deal
With your brother, the foul *Enrico*,
Who my estates did steal.'

'I'll renounce my claim to Ravenswood
And let him keep the land,
In return for a far more precious thing,
Lucia dear, your hand.'

'Though landless, we will both work hard
And, in a joint account
With the Royal Bank of Scotland,
We will watch our savings mount.'

But Lucia has another plan
To achieve fulfilment quicker,
'Let us plight our troths at once,'
She says, 'and of leesome bliss mak siccer.'

They exchange their rings and make their vows
Of fidelity for life,
Which under Scots law means, of course,
They're as good as man and wife.

But now *Edgardo* has to leave,
For he hears the ferry's whistle,
Which calls him to French *Fleur-de-Lys*,
Away from Scottish thistle.

'I'll write you letters, dear,' he cries,
'And mail them back first class,
To keep you fully posted
Of all that comes to pass.'

This promise, crucial to the plot,
Was too readily accepted.
Lucia hadn't realized
That her mail was intercepted.

Act I, Scene 3

The Scene is *Enrico's* chamber,
Where a plot has now been hatched
To appeal to family loyalty
And have *Lucia* matched

With *Arturo*, who'll soon be in the hall,
Where the guests e'en now assemble,
And she will be persuaded,
Her revulsion to dissemble.

Already she's been softened up,
For she's received no letter.
Raimondo's stolen every one.
(A chaplain should know better.)

Worse still, he know's *Edgardo's* hand
And a letter he has written,
Purporting to be from *Edgardo*
To some flighty French sex-kitten,

The letter is in French, of course,
(*Raimondo* is no fool.)
But like any well-bred Scottish maid,
Lucia learnt French at school.

So when she's shown this forgery,
She believes she's been betrayed,
And that her beloved *Edgardo*
Prefers another maid.

She cries, 'Alas! This is too much.
My whole life has been blighted.
But *Arturo* still I cannot wed,
For *Edgardo* and I have plighted'

'Our troths to one another,
So we're as good as wed.
While he's alive no other man
Can legally share my bed.'

'Come, put aside these scruples,'
Her brother, *Enrico*, roars,
'Surely you know the mortgagees
Are waiting at the doors?'

'If we don't get *Arturo*'s gowd
And his stacks of shining siller,
We will be, to use a sailor's phrase,
Up the creek without a tiller.'

'You will no longer drink your tay
Out of a china tassie,
But from a mug of earthenware,
Like a common working lassie.'

'All right,' replies *Lucia*,
'If that is what you wish,
I'll sacrifice myself as bait,
To catch this golden fish.'

'But warn *Arturo* my temper's short.
It won't take much to trigger me,
Especially under the added strain
Of having committed bigamy.'

Raimondo's pleased to know that cash
Will soon be in the kitty,
To pay his stipend, so he sings
A pompous little ditty,

'Your sacrifice, *Lucia*,
The Angels will record,
And God will see that, when you die,
 You gain your just reward.'

Lucia isn't much impressed
By thoughts of heavenly guerdon,
And says, 'Excuse me, I must dress
To take up my earthly burden.'

Act I, Scene 4

The scene is the hall of Ravenswood,
Its splendour is spread before us,
And Enrico's retainers and his friends
Are singing a welcoming chorus

For *Arturo*, who has just arrived,
By sea on a nearby beach,
And is most relieved to think that he
Has marriage within his reach.

The retainers greet him joyfully,
And give three hearty cheers,
For his gold will pay their wages,
Which are six months in arrears.

The creditors all look forward
To the money they are owed,
And say, 'Where are your treasure-chests?
We'll help you to unload.'

Enrico's friends are also glad,
That he'll soon be in the black,
So that when they ask him out to dine,
He'll be able to ask them back.

Arturo says, 'I'm very glad
To be able to help restore
Your family fortunes. But where's *Lucia*?
I thought she'd be at the door.'

Enrico replies, 'She'll be down quite soon.
She was always a slowish dresser.
And I didn't want to hurry her up,
As I thought it might distress 'er.'

For she's recently been, I am sorry to say,
(Though I fear it has got to be said,)
Just a little bit, (how can I put it, old man?)
Not terribly keen to be wed.'

'And it isn't because she thinks you're a wimp,
Nor that you have bad breath,
But I think it's because she's still upset
By her mother's recent death.'

'So if she seems a bit distraught,
Please take it in good part.
Ah! Here she comes, *Arturo*,
The wedding now can start.'

Lucia, who, as we all can see,
Is more than a bit distraught,
Says, 'Hi *Arturo*! You don't look quite
Such a wimp as I had thought.'

'And although, quite frankly, I'd far prefer
To remain a maid unspliced,
I am prepared, for my family's sake,
To be thus sacrificed.

But, when she signs the contract,
She whispers, beneath her breath,
'This is no marriage contract,
But a warrant for my death.'

At this, a scuffle is heard outside
And *Edgardo* enters, ranting,
And says, 'What has been going on?
Why all this gallivanting?'

He's travel-stained and has a sword,
On a belt around his waist.
He's evidently heard the news
And returned from France in haste.

This is the cue for the great sextet,
When everyone sings to explain,
Exactly what their sentiments are,
then repeat them over again.

Edgardo says, 'I am betrayed.
She is married to another.
But still I think she shows remorse
And I find that I still love 'er.'

Enrico says, 'I am incensed,
Edgardo is a twister.
But perhaps I have been just a bit
Unkind to my dear sister.

Raimondo says, 'Oh! Woe is me!
She hangs on by a thread.
It's difficult to help a girl
Who wishes she were dead.'

Arturo and *Alisa*
Then do their level best
To echo all the sentiments
The others have expressed.

Enrico and *Arturo*
Then swiftly draw their swords
And say, '*Edgardo*, please depart
Or your blood will stain the boards.'

'We are both of us good swordsmen
And valiant Scottish souls.
You can either leave at once, on foot,
Or feet-first, full of holes.'

Edgardo draws his sword as well,
And says, 'I fear not death,
And both of you will follow me,
When I draw my dying breath.'

Raimondo says, 'This is no way
To start a wedding feast.
Before we fall to fighting,
Let us toast the bride at least.'

'It's very impolite to fight,'
He unctuously preaches,
'Before they've cut the wedding cake
And finished all the speeches.'

Arturo's glad to be told to stop,
And puts his sword away,
For he cannot bear the sight of blood
And is useless at sword-play.

Edgardo and *Lucia*
Return each other's rings.
He reproaches her for betraying him,
As bitterly he sings.

He throws away his sword and says,
'You may kill me where I stand.
I have nothing left to live for,
Now I've lost *Lucia*'s hand.'

But no-one takes his offer up,
So he sadly slinks away,
To curse *Lucia*'s family
And rue her wedding day.

Act II, Scene 1

The scene is in the Wolf's Crag Tower,
Where *Edgardo* has his squat.
He's come back from the wedding feast,
To brood upon his lot.

A thunderstorm has broken out,
Like the storm within his breast,
So he's surprised to hear the sound
Of an unexpected guest.

It's *Enrico*, who has left the feast.
To his rage the storm adds fuel.
To *Edgardo* he says, 'Let's have it out,
I challenge you to a duel.'

'To be held at dawn to-morrow morn,
Near the tombs of Ravenswood.'
Edgardo thinks it's a great idea,
And replies, 'OK that's good.'

'I couldn't think of a better place
For the vengeance I am sworn to.
My father's ghost can cheer me on,
To the fate that I was born to.'

'And if by chance you kill me too,
No tears need my friends shed.
Life holds no pleasure for me now
Lucia's in *Arturo*'s bed.'

So both of them look forward
Too duelling at first light,
And *Enrico* goes back to Ravenswood,
Through the dark and stormy night.

Act II, Scene 2

The scene is Ravenswood's hall again,
Where the hour is getting late.
The guests are dancing jigs and reels
And the merriment is great.

Raimondo enters, gasping,
And for silence makes a call.
When the guests behold his pallor,
A hush falls on the hall.

'Oh cease your merriment.' he cries,
'A crime has been committed.
Lucia, with his own sharp sword,
Her husband has just spitted.'

'I'm a student of psychiatry
And I think she's flipped her lid,
And can probably no longer tell
Her ego from her id.'

'At this stage I can only make
A tentative diagnosis,
But it looks like a rather serious case
Of post-marital Psychosis.'

Lucia enters just behind.
Her blood-stained hands she's ringing,
And though she's clearly at death's door,
It doesn't affect her singing.

She warbles on for quite some time,
(The mad-scene it is called.)
While the guests stand by, transfixed with awe,
And are clearly quite appalled.

It seems that she has no idea
What has happened to *Arturo*,
But sings about *Edgardo*
And *amore in futuro*.

Enrico enters hurriedly,
Looks round the stricken room,
And asks, 'Is this the truth I hear?
Has *Lucia* slain the groom?'

'You are a glaikit gowk,' he greets,
'You should be sairly chid.'
But *Raimondo* interrupts and says,
'Can't you see she's flipped her lid?'

Enrico replies, 'I see all now.
I have wronged my luckless sister.
Edgardo was a lover true
And not, as I thought, a twister.'

'It is too late for recompense.
She sighs for sweet release.
So lead her to her chamber
And let her die in peace.'

Raimondo and *Normanno*
Are left in the silent hall
And naturally the former
Blames the latter for it all.

Raimondo says, 'You struck the first
Of the sparks that lit this fire.'
Conveniently forgetting
That he, too, did conspire,

And 'twas he who forged the letter,
That sealed *Lucia*'s fate.
Though a chaplain, he was a thoroughly foul,
Hypocritical reprobate.

Act II, Scene 3

Now we have reached the final scene,
Set near the tombs at night.
Edgardo is there already,
Although it is not yet light.

He sings of his family's rotten luck
And thinks of *Lucia* lying,
As he thinks she is, in *Arturo*'s arms,
Though actually she's dying.

Just then there come from the castle gates
A group of retainers, crying.
'Whatever has happened ?' he says to them,
'Is somebody up there dying?'

'It is *Lucia*.' they sadly reply,
And tell him the doleful story,
Omitting none of the details,
Which are really rather gory.

Raimondo enters at this point,
And says, 'You are left alone.
The bell is tolling. Can't you hear?
Her soul is to heaven flown.'

Edgardo pulls a dagger out,
And though they say, 'Please don't.'
Says, 'I will go to join her there.
We will meet as was our wont.'

'Although our love on earth has been
Irreparably blighted,
 I will plunge this blade into my heart
And we'll be re-united.'

Raimondo and the rest shed tears,
As he sings with his dying breaths,
And the curtain falls upon the last
Of three untimely deaths.

THE SERIOUS BIT

The four poems in this section were written in 1994. 'D Day' was prompted by the ceremonies marking the 50th anniversary of the Normandy landings. 'Cana of Galilee' puts a new, but I hope not irreverent, slant on the well-known Bible story. 'To Cease upon the Midnight' and 'Afterthought' speak for themselves.

CANA OF GALILEE

A Pharisee drew the young man aside and said
'I see you know your wine
And with my help you could make plenty of bread.
I'll look after marketing and finance,
And with you looking after
Production and quality control
The competition won't stand a chance.
All the money-changers know I'm thrifty,
And after deducting usury and my consultancy fees,
We'll split the profits fifty-fifty.
I'll get a scribe to draw up a contract for you to sign
And then you can start turning out the wine.'

The young man said, 'Fine!
My dad had been trying to get me to start a new religion,
But it would probably never have got off the ground.
I am sure your proposition is more sound.
Everyone should use their talents
And although I have no formal qualification,
I do have a talent for vinifcation.
But my dad probably won't see it that way
And will tell me to go into the wilderness to pray.'

The Pharisee said, 'You're a good Jewish lad,
So try not to disappoint your dad.
Why not cut him in?
When the business grows
We'll need some help with personnel and admin.'

The young man said, 'I'll ask him,
But he'll probably be rather cross
And tell me that I'm a dead loss.'

The Pharisee said, 'I understand your position.
Some fathers use their sons to further their own ambition,
Instead of allowing them to come to fruition
By following their own intuition.'

The young man said, 'You're very perceptive.
To other people's ideas my dad's not very receptive.
I'll try to make him listen to my spiel,
But he probably won't so I'll have to call off our deal.'

The Pharisee said, 'I know how you feel.
In the wine trade a lad like you could have gone far,
But if you do decide to start a new religion instead,
I've got good media contacts and could help you with PR.
We could launch it with a feature in the 'Bethlehem Star'.

D DAY

An Old Oundelian Remembers.

At morning prayers in 1942 our grave Headmaster read
The names of missing and of dead.
We new boys bowed our heads - it seemed the thing to do.
We heard the names of men we never knew.

In 1944 there was no need to feign
Our grief. We felt the pain,
Not just because we'd older grown.
Among the names were boys that we had known.

TO CEASE UPON THE MIDNIGHT

TO CEASE UPON THE MIDNIGHT

In the brave days of yore when an old man lay dying
And his family around the four-poster stood crying,
They would send for a priest to give Unction Extreme,
For they hadn't then heard of a Life Support Team.

Now, when an old man is quite ready to die,
Some officious young doctor will probably cry,
'Men are often not nearly as ill as they seem.
Though he's ninety I'll send for a Life Support Team.'

'We'll not ask his permission. It's not his affair.
He's unconscious and so he won't know they are there.
In fact he will probably not even dream
That he's under the care of a Life Support Team.'

'We can keep him alive for a good week or two,
Though he's bound to die sometime, old men always do,
But our hospital gains in professional esteem,
By showing it's got a good Life Support Team.'

So when even one step becomes too much to climb,
And I've told the same joke for the four hundredth time,
When the ferry lies ready at the bank of the stream,
Please, Family, don't send for a Life Support Team.

Just help me aboard to a comfy deck-chair,
And give me the money for the ferryman's fare.
Shed tears if you must and then leave me to dream,
Till I'm out of the reach of the Life Support Team.

AFTERTHOUGHT

But if death should assail me before my good time,
If I'm victim of accident, mishap or crime,
For goodness sake, woman, don't stand there and scream,
But send for the very best Life Support Team.